Praise for W

"This collection is a powerful outpouring of hurt and healing. *When Silence Found Her Voice* is an authentic, poignant, and raw examination of trauma, self-awareness, and faith. Through vivid and insightful craftsmanship, Bogdan evokes the full spectrum of human emotion and gives an honest voice to the messiness of reconstruction. Her uncompromising vulnerability will leave you unearthed, unashamed, and remade."
—S. C. Says, author of *Golden Brown Skin*

When Silence

Found Her Voice

When Silence Found Her Voice

By Taylour R. Bogdan

This is a work of fiction.
No character in this work is a real person.

Paperback ISBN: 979-8-9892621-0-6
Ebook ISBN: 979-8-9892621-1-3

Photo copyright 2022 © Amani Sodiq-Odunaiya.
Photos used by permission.

Editor and print book layout designer:
Carolina VonKampen, CarolinaVonKampen.com
Ebook designer: Lorie DeWorken
Photography model: Taylour R. Bogdan
Photographer: Amani Sodiq-Odunaiya,
IncendiPhotography.com
Cover designer: Brandon Hilliard, bhilli1221@gmail.com

A Letter to You

Dear Reader,

I'm so happy you're here with me and ready to explore the world of poetry.

Please know this poetry collection may have triggering themes. So always take care of yourself first by practicing self-care if triggering moments surface.

I believe there is strength when we share our stories and listen with compassion. I hope this collection inspires you to find your voice and to speak your truth—however that may look.

It means so much to me you're on this journey with me. I hope to hear your story one day.

—Taylour

Acknowledgments

My husband, thank you for your unconditional love, support, guidance, and encouragement. Being loved by you is pure magic, and I'm elated we get to do life together.

Thank you to the people in my life who made space for me to grow, explore, and transform into the woman I am today. I see you and am truly thankful to have you in my life.

words danced from my lips

Piercing the Unknown

my silence broke
as the words danced
from my lips
casting a spell
your body turned to stone
while your soul grieved
for my innocence
I was no longer a little girl
who played in the sugar plum
patch, but a child forced
into an adult world.

Violated

you touched me
I said nothing

you touched me
a child

you touched me
I died

you touched me

you touched me

you touched me

piece by bony piece
my soul is ripped away

I never gave you permission

but you continued
to claw your way to my core

Descend into the Empty

my mouth opens to scream
nothing comes out
my ears bleed
I'm silenced
into
oblivion

Looking for My Salvation

sinners welcome
sin is sin
sadly
not on these holy grounds
leader of the congregation
judgment in a place of holiness
is God not here?
cursed
judged
refuge I seek
home I do not find
I am abandoned
banished
in a world
where sins are not the same

A Physical Response

my nipple he squeezed
betrayed by my body
my tongue he bit
betrayed by my body
my vagina he fingered
betrayed by my body
betrayed by my body
betrayed
by
my
body

I would not become a faded memory

Alone, Together

a teenager
first lust blooms
sex
(it's a simple request)
he begins to touch me
fingertips searing
I can't
I say no
his pride is hurt
"Don't you want me?"
he begs.
I can't do this.
He glides his fingers
in between my thighs
fear wins—I pull away
"What am I doing wrong?"
Nothing.
"Do you want to see me?"
He begins to unbutton his jeans.
"NO!" My scream escapes.
Fear won. I leave.
My virginity intact.

Silent Thoughts

molestation.
it's my fault.

again and again.

and again.

and again.

eternity goes by.
will it ever end?

I was silenced.

I *was* silenced. .

I was *silenced* . . .

My Innocence Appropriated

Father Time is no longer a friend, but a foe.

I glare at him
with hate in my eyes
and agony in my heart.

"Why? Why now?" I scream.

His glazed eyes stare right through me.
I do not exist in his time.
He has come to take another.

I try to stop him,
but he is a silhouette of a man.

I fall through him.

He takes her hand,
whispering, "It is time."

I scream
I kick
I cry
but to no avail.

Father Time has come and gone,
leaving me with empty years to ponder.
"Why? Why now?"

Shards of Destruction

shards of glass spray the floor
red drips
from their tips
the pain slowly dissipates
numbness conquers

I welcome it.

A Belief's Sorrows

the apple of my eye
the golden fruit—forever forbidden
that's what the church preaches

ignorance is bliss
thou shall not eat
closer to temptation
the snake strikes

and I'm cast out for my body
being soiled when I was only
a child.

my innocence and faith
gone.

I embrace my choice

A Titillated Brand

his fingers scorch my skin
hot coals
in the pit of my stomach

I want to throw up
I can't make a sound

it was the little secret
damning me

he titillated me
still his fingers branded me

I want to scream
knives pull at my throat
I can't make a sound
the walls are thin
they'll hear us

it was the little secret
damning me

my voice—

silenced.

A Cold Irony

one by one the members gather.
their condolences sickening as they
pass by with their judgmental glares
I stare as my grief overwhelms
for now I know my childhood is no longer filled with
princes or knights coming to my rescue
even though adults continue to play
follow the leader
tossing dirt into the grave one by one
I watch as my innocence
descends into the earth—entombed

Unmasking

I thought I was forever bound to you

my false protector

you taught the little secret

filth filled my guts
fear ruled my heart

you were not my savior

you are bigot
you are molester
you are liar
you are hate
you are coward
you are disgrace

Everlasting Evanescent

you did not know me
you pillaged my innocence

a priceless treasure

you took advantage
you stole my power
you scavenged my essence

isolated in the dark

you touched
you licked
you pinched
you sacrificed my identity

in an eternal second

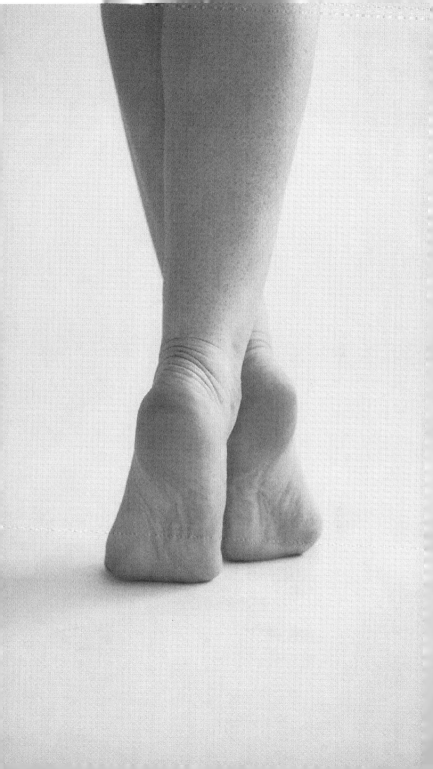

Prophecy

fury spews from my soul
hate consumes me
my body convulses

the Fates have spoken
it is written
it shall come to pass—

death,
I will welcome.

Despair

the era of innocence desecrated
the world turned dark
the princess imprisoned in her tower
the dragon of death prowled

creating havoc
destroying every beautiful dream
damaging every fantasy of home
dispelling every hope for Prince Charming

her life
her soul
her purity

burning
turning to ash

Volition

the sea's vast depths—
I lose myself in the cold waters.

the waves crashing down
washing me of my sins.

the beat of the waves
parallel with my pulse

the sea splits
I am naked

air hits my lungs
I rasp and cough.

the eye of the storm has come.
judgment is here.

two paths
I embrace my choice.

Finding My Way

you did this to me

your lies
your torment

I bled to death

heartless
soulless
immoral

my naked body
exposed to the world
I was to be forgotten
so you groomed your next victim

flames erupted
beneath my lifeless body

I would not be forgotten
I would not become a faded memory
the world will be clothed in truth

my honor
my victory
my justice

will be known

Hope

from the depths of my despair
golden light bursts through the clouds
and rains from the sky
God is here
I am not alone

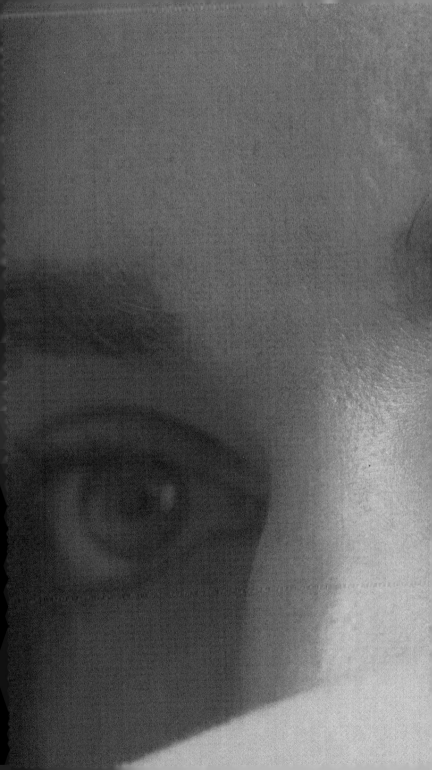

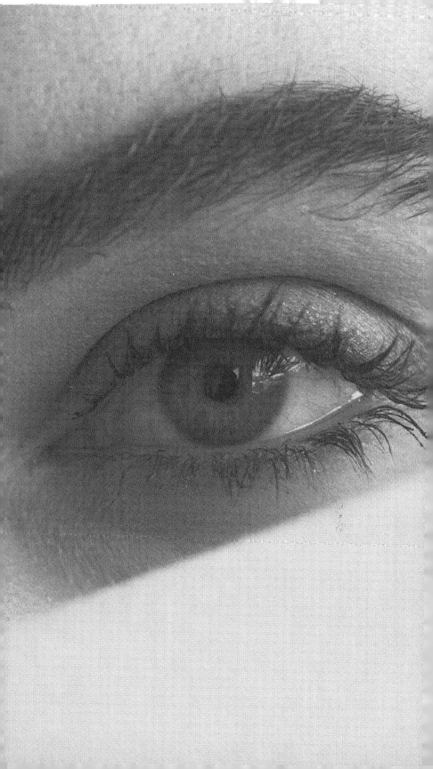

Preparing for Battle

hellfire swarms my thoughts
smoke engulfs my lungs
blood drips from my limbs
the truth seeps from my lips
a warrior I become
as the war begins

my   sovereignty   reclaimed

Mayhem

steel clashes, sparks scatter
anger bubbles spilling silently

armies slowly circle
face-to-face with dragon

do I slice through with fury
or prevail with truth?

a crossroad looms
my weapon's hilt in hand

scribbling the lyrics
my siren call sings

releasing my soul
from captivity

Fulfilling a Prophecy

air choked with smoke
flames rage
hope vanishes
destruction complete

I collapse
my hair singed
my flesh blistered
my skin bloodied
my clothes burned
I scream

fate comes for me

I burn.

I fall.

I stand.

fate has not won . . .

yet.

Liberation

the damage is done
the ashes
a quilt of despair
wraps around the era of adolescence
I feel nothing
I am numb
shattered
my pale skin
stained with the coal-like powder
the spark flickers
slowly dying
"It is not your fault"
whispers my fairy godmother
the phrase repeats again and again
"It is not your fault"

I feel the burn within
I stand
I rise above destruction
I rise above lies
I rise above the dragon
I rise above the ashes
my prison no more
I soar toward the heavens
engulfed with liberation
enveloped by tranquility
I am free

Reverberation

in a sea of people
my lips part

crisp fall air permeates
my senses

lightning cracks
my veins spark

silence breaks
my voice heard

my sovereignty
reclaimed

Acceptance

I was abused
by a loved one
I was abused
by a damaged one
I was abused
by a deceitful one
I was abused
by someone

I am saved
by the Eternal One
I am loved
by the Eternal One
I am protected
by the Eternal One
I am home
with the Eternal One

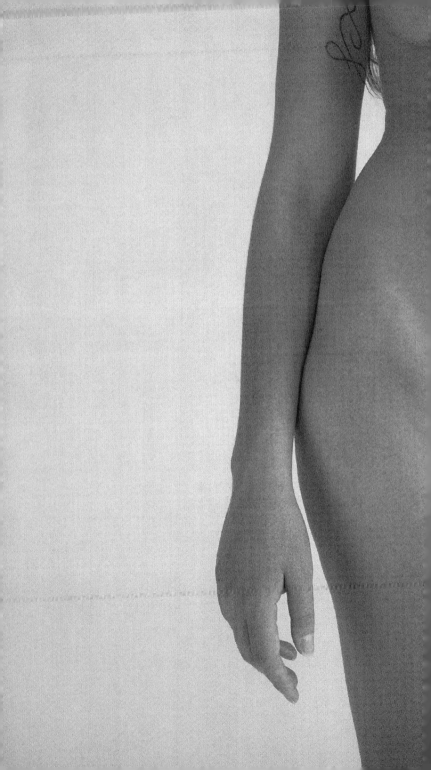

Shattering

entombed in stone
the darkness consumes
my facade cracks
his claws grasp tighter
a piece falls
light shines through
he screams
the earth shakes
my stone prison shatters
the crypt vanishes
light illuminates
he is no more
my soul soars with serenity

Shine

golden glow
cascading,
illuminating the gloom
angelic harmony
banishes my demons
I am the knight
who found her light

Embracing My Art

I never asked God
why me?
I always asked God
what now?
my fingers would twitch
my hand itched
ink befriended
the parchment
my spirit was inked
by the words etched
on my skin
a gift of divinity

Explorer

I have learned
when I trust myself
my purpose is clear
my talents beam
writing and connecting
galaxies
sharing stories with
mysticism
giving permission to explore
and learning
we are not alone
we are not our past
we are pure
we are love
we are exotic
and made with magic

a woman cloaked in courage

Affirmation

I am:
a woman cloaked in courage
my flesh armed in truth
I am protected by faith
my salvation
my coat of arms
the knight, I deemed

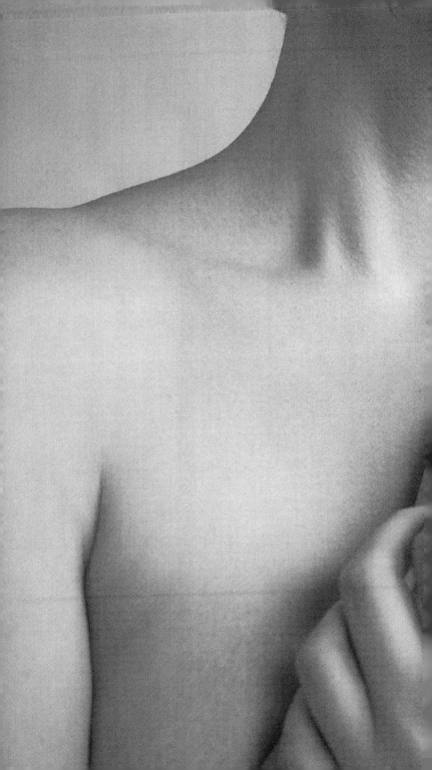

my soul soars with serenity

I Am a Woman

reclaiming my divinity—my power, my femininity.
scarred and bruised—I refuse to be broken.
I rise. resilient and bold—hear my battle cry.
the revelation your power no longer exists.
I resist your terror and twist your lies
into truth. I weave your brand with strands of gold.
turning the curve of my breasts,
the plains of my stomach,
the arc of my hips,
and the valley between my thighs
into a seraphic tapestry. my body knows
the history, and the victory is mine
as I rise

A Celestial Twist

Sometimes the world is
cruel,
but so is
my guardian angel.

Final Battle

the dragon surges toward me
the guards race to protect me
"No," I say, "this is my fight."
face to face
I stand
the beast
the devil himself
claws scrape the ground
sword is unsheathed
steel meets flesh
the dragon's head
severed. my monster—
dead.

Dark Beauty

rain drizzles
mixing ash and flecks of gold
beauty found in the rubble
a halcyon feather
floating down as
a pyroclastic flow
poured from my veins
I awaken
walking the auric streets

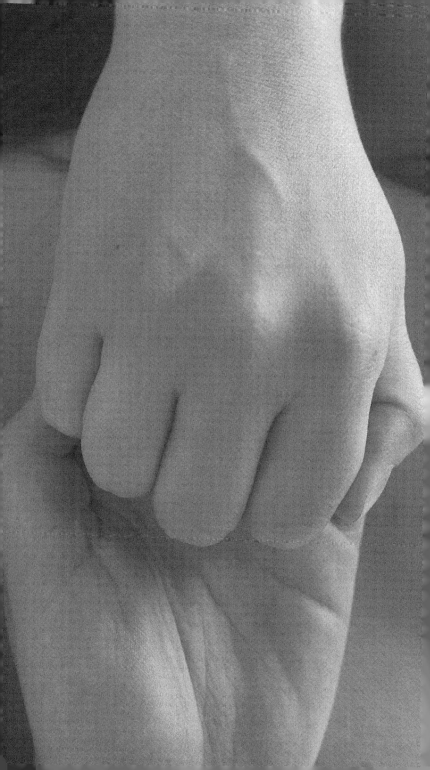

Survivor

I found a sword
and conquered the world
I am fearless
my demons are vanquished
my sorrows conquered
a golden phoenix
I am a voice
for the silent
protector of innocence

Accepting the Gift

the apple of His eye
I am His
God is here
alone I never will be
my spirit
healed
He gives me wings
the golden quill
the magic erupts
I am forever changed

Transformation

God's whispers of freedom
breathing life
waking the mystical bird
my golden wings open
the cruel ashes fall
I take flight
God's whispers of love
filling the empty crevices
fall I will not
my golden wings soar
God's whispers of home
the enchanting light shines
the tears run dry
life is beauty
this is phoenix anew
this is me

Metamorphosis

charcoal chains turn
into golden silk
the truth
revealed
victim
no more
survivor
I am

Strength

from the ashes of death
the fire of life rises
ascending above the debris
quelling the grief
gleaming
through the era of womanhood
embracing the power
vanquishing the enemy
the dragon of death—hades welcomes
rising above hate's cruel afflictions
courage to fight
freedom reigns
a protector of the weak
a voice for the speechless
a phoenix knight
the throne
is mine

Purpose

her claws firmly planted
to protect and defend
the imprisoned
her strong legs
carrying her body
through life's changes
her powerful wings
lifting her toward the heavens
sweeping the skies
her blue eyes forever
seeking truth
the window to the soul
her beak eternally her voice
she speaks honorably
her story known
she is a golden phoenix
she is me

Finding Peace

the healing began
when I confronted
my fears.
the fears left my soul
withered on paper
the dry ink
finalized their departure

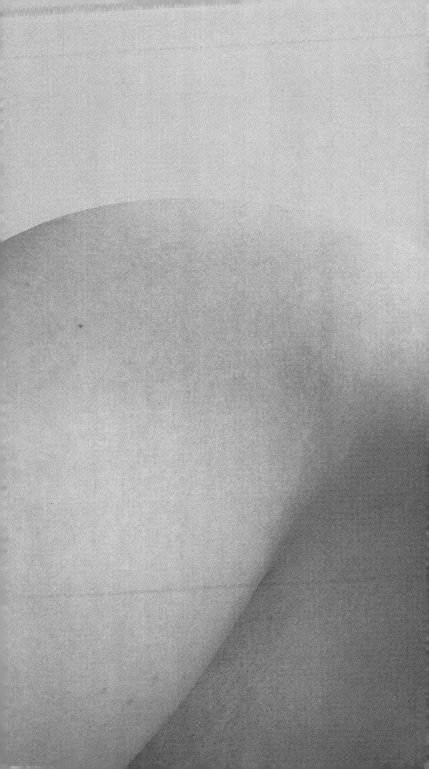

Be You

in this world of hate
know you are kind
in this world of abandonment
know you are not alone
in this world of abuse
know you are not broken
you are intelligent
you are strong
you are courageous
you are important
you are who you're
supposed to be

I am reborn

A New Day

the daybreak
golden hour shines
the eternal warmth
washes over the valley
basking in the light
it's a brand-new day
the broken pieces
healed
fear is vanquished
replaced
by hope and faith
it's a brand-new day

Confidence

Learn to be
sophisticated
like silk,
wild like
a flame.

Finding My Salvation

they fear what they don't try
to understand; there—they set flames
to my flesh. Golden flames lick my naked skin.
my soul embraces their warmth and
laughter erupts from my throat.
the amber blaze breathes life
into my soul—for it is my
salvation. My body burns
as my voice rises from the ash
the earth quakes with truth
she hears my call
sprouting her green veins
red dahlias bloom
turning to the moonlit sky
as she cries—honoring my strength
and knowing I am safe. I am reborn.

A New Beginning

I found myself wandering aimlessly
I had won the war yet my pain
still seethed within. My heart still ached—
my body fevered with shame. Salt water
scorches my cheeks as it trickles down
over my lashes. I continue to walk, no destination.
My eyes blur—I fall through the break in the tree
line. I gasp as something small and light touches
my hand. Petals; pink petals blanket
the field. The only pop of color to recover after it
was smothered. A smile erupts and laughter
bubbles over. Cherry blossoms bloom,
their smell invigorating. I inhale their perfume,
reaching the depths of my soul. Their deep magic
teaching me their way to forgiveness—I accept.
My pain. Obliterated. The liberation—
peaceful.

Connecting

in a time of need
spoken words fail
the fountain pen speaks
ink and parchment meet
invoking warmth and wonder
truth and peace ignite
the secrets burn and
justice rages
across the page
my truth
my story
the written words sail
changing history
reaching
across the seas—uniting
thousands of survivors
and advocates
the tides are changing
bringing us together
we will prevail

Finding My Way Back to Me

As the last drop of the black ink dries
the mulberry tree sways her branches
she caresses my cheek, comforting me—
I lay down my sword. "Thank you,"
I whisper as the pages fly
toward the sky. Reaching places
beyond my imagination. The words
they carry married with
pain and joy
grief and anger
fear and courage
peace and forgiveness.
Their magic releases me
from the burdens and brings me back to
sugar plum patches and
pixie dust.

About the Author

Taylour R. Bogdan graduated with her associate's degree in mass communication and a bachelor's degree in English with a focus in creative writing and minor in journalism.

She has written this collection of poems to inspire hope and to help others feel less alone as they learn to heal from their pain.

She believes everyone has a story to share and there is no better way to connect than learning from each other.

Connect with Taylour on Instagram at @t.r.bogdan.

Made in the USA
Columbia, SC
28 June 2024

37715000R00050